DON'T GO PAYING THE NURSING HOME

How Californians Can Protect Their Homes, Cash, and Retirement Accounts

by Karl Kim, CFP®, CLTC

MW00669318

Copyright © 2013 Retirement Planning Advisors, Inc. All rights reserved. No part of this book may be reproduced in any form, electronic or mechanical, including photocopying and recording, or by any information storage or retrieval system, without prior written permission from the copyright owner, except as allowed by federal law.

Printed in the United States of America
First Edition printed February 2013
10 9 8 7 6 5 4 3 2 1

ISBN 978-0-9889026-1-9

For permission requests, contact:
Retirement Planning Advisors, Inc.
16700 Valley View Ave., Suite 160
La Mirada, CA   90638

This book is meant to provide an overview of complex subject matter. However, the contents may not be sufficient for dealing with every person's particular circumstances. Persons using this publication do so with the understanding that neither Karl Kim nor Retirement Planning Advisors, Inc. are engaged in or rendering legal, accounting, financial, tax advice or other professional services. The information published herein should not be relied on as a substitute for the advice of an attorney, tax advisor, or financial advisor. This publication is not meant to provide legal, accounting, financial or tax advice. Under no circumstances will Karl Kim of Retirement Planning Advisors, Inc. be liable for any consequential damages that result from the use of, or the inability to use, any or part of the information contained in this book. No guarantees are implied or written as to the protection of assets or income for the qualification of benefits. The author is not liable for any omissions or errors in the material. Senate Bill 483 was passed on September 27, 2008 and is pending implementation as of this time. This is California's implementation of the Deficit Reduction Act of 2005. This may materially impact future planning.

TABLE OF CONTENTS

Acknowledgements

Dennis Mochizuki, Esq. and Glenn Nakatani, Esq. are the legal minds I always fall back on. As experienced trust and probate attorneys, they are also knowledgeable about Medi-Cal planning.

Thank you to those at Keiro Senior HealthCare: Shawn Miyake, President and CEO; Dianne Kujubu Belli, CAO; and Gene Kanamori, Director of Human Resources. Staff members of the Intermediate Care Facility also provided invaluable insight, including: Beverly Ito, Administrator; and Rie Sera, Business Office Manager.

Special consideration to Marilee Driscoll, author of *Idiot's Guide to Long Term Care Planning* and the editor of my first project, *Don't Be A Burden*. Thanks for all of your help, guidance and knowledge.

Finally, many thanks to my wife Nancy, my daughter Courtney, and my son Brandon.

1 – The Long-Term Care Tsunami

A tsunami can travel undetected for thousands and thousands of miles. Its unseen power and fury can cause massive destruction once it comes ashore.

A healthcare crisis such as a stroke or heart attack is much like a tsunami. It happens without warning. When it happens, severe financial, emotional, health and family distress take place.

On the other hand, illnesses like Alzheimer's, dementia, or Parkinson's can happen slowly. Our need for help as we get older can sneak up on us, but the results of distress are the same.

Sadly, most people are overtaken by the waves of issues when dealing with a long-term care crisis, and they drown slowly. Many actually spend more time planning a vacation than planning for their eventual long-term care needs.

Ever hear "It won't happen to me"? Well, think again.

Let's face it, we are all getting older. According to the U.S. Census Bureau, by 2050 there will be 88.5 million seniors. That's over 20% of the U.S. population.

One of the reasons that the tsunami is so impactful is that it is always accompanied by what is referred to as *Information Overload*.

In the old days we would to go to the library to research a subject. We would speak with family, friends and professional advisors. These advisors knew us, knew our situation.

Today, with the internet, research can give you millions of hits. The problem is, this information is not personalized and may actually be detrimental if followed. Consider the following:

- How can someone read all of the material they find at various websites?
- What applies to your situation and what does not?
- Is the article factual or just made up?
- Can you determine the authority of the article you have read?

Information overload causes confusion, frustration and stress!

This book will help educate and inform you. It will filter out the unnecessary information that doesn't apply in California. It will present information in a manner that is easy to understand.

Our job is to make your life easier and less stressful. We will walk with you through this government bureaucracy and you'll be amazed at how quickly you'll start to get a better picture of the system.

Let's begin by ascertaining one important fact. The long-term care plan for many parents consists of presuming that their adult children will take care of them. Good idea, right? WRONG!

Most adult children can't even take care of themselves. They're busy raising their own family. They're taking their own kids to school, ballet, sports and participating in all of the things that kids want to do. They are being pulled in a dozen different directions.

It's not that they don't love their parents, it's just that they don't have the time or energy to help.

But that's okay because there are simple and easy steps you can take to be prepared. This book help you learn them and get organized.

By the time you're done reading, you will know how to protect all of your hard-earned money and your home so that you can keep them for your spouse and family. You won't be a burden on your spouse, children or family. They won't be subject to stress while trying to figure all of this out.

Wouldn't that be great?

Here's another fact. In addition to thinking, "It won't happen to me," one-third of all seniors mistakenly believe that Medicare and their health insurance will pay for their long-term care services.

That's because people don't know the difference between short-term and long-term care. We're going to go through this shortly. Just be aware of this: **the high cost of long-term care will suck you under and drown you!**

People are absolutely flabbergasted by the astronomical cost of long-term care when something goes awry. Grab a seat and hold on because we're going to review the results of a 2011 survey by Prudential Insurance.

A private room in a nursing home costs:

- $312 per day in San Francisco ($113,880 per year).
- $227 per day in Los Angeles ($82,855 per year).
- $286 per day in San Diego ($104,390 per year).

That's twice as much as sending your high school graduate to one year at a private college.

Assisted living is like a senior apartment, but there is a dining room where three meals a day are served.

The average annual rate for assisted living is:

- $33,012 in San Francisco.
- $29,424 in Los Angeles.
- $27,648 in San Diego.

How does someone pay for this? Doesn't the government help?

Sadly the answer is **NO**. This is all on you.

Why hasn't anyone told you about this? Well, the government keeps a lot of secrets… and this is perhaps the biggest one of all.

Fortunately, you are reading this book. By the time you are done, you **will** crack the code.

What about home care? It's cheaper isn't it? Maybe not.

The average hourly rates for the services of a licensed home health care agency in various parts of California are:

- $25 per hour in San Francisco.
- $23 per hour in Los Angeles.
- $30 per hour in San Diego.

Let's do the math. $25 per hour times 24 hours in a day times 365 days a year equals **$219,000**. So, when we compare apples to apples and oranges to oranges, home care is **more expensive** than a nursing home.

But unlike a nursing home, we can lower that cost by reducing the number of hours of service. Family members can also pitch in to give the healthcare providers time off.

Now do you understand why you need to be able to swim with your eyes open? You don't have to drown under the long-term care tsunami. This book is your life jacket.

Taking Care of Someone is a Piece of Cake

People severely underestimate the emotional, physical and time burden that is associated with care giving.

The stress is never ending, 24 hours a day, 365 days a year, day in, day out. Lifting someone into the bathtub, feeding them, getting them onto the toilet, giving them their medicine, stopping them from wandering away, making sure they don't leave the stove on so the house doesn't burn down, are all part and parcel to care giving.

Unless someone has actually been in a care giving situation, it is next to impossible to tell someone about the experience.

Taking care of a friend or family member is not a piece of cake. It is exhausting. I have actually seen cases where the caregiver passes away before the person that they are taking care of does.

Don't let this be you!

2 – What's the Difference Between Medicare, Medicaid and Medi-Cal?

To answer this question, you have to understand the difference between short- and long-term care.

Short-term care is also called rehabilitative, or rehab care. You might want to think of it as "get better care."

After someone leaves the hospital, they need to get better, so they go to a rehab facility. This is otherwise known as a nursing home, and the purpose is to get the person well enough to be able to function in a home setting.

Once in this nursing home, the person is monitored. When he or she is no longer getting better (and obviously not getting worse) their condition is labeled as **stable**.

At this point, short-term or rehab care ends and long-term care begins.

If you are 65 or older, Medicare pays for short-term, or rehab care.

However, no matter what you may think, know this: **Medicare does not pay for long-term care!**

Some people get confused about this because rehab care is provided in a **nursing home**.

So is long-term care.

It just makes sense for them both to be covered, but they are not. What many Californians don't know is that even though the services they receive are in the same place, one type is considered short-term and the other is long-term.

Short-term care is paid for under Medicare – long-term care is not.

Medicare pays for rehab care after a senior has been in the hospital for at least 3 straight days and is then released to a nursing home. The first 20 days of short-term care is paid for by Medicare.

Payment for days 21 through 100 varies, depending on what type of Medicare supplement insurance or HMO you have.

Take a look at the chart.

Days	You Pay	Medicare Pays
1-20	Nothing	Everything
21-100	$148 x 80 days = $11,840	Balance
100+	Everything	Nothing

Remember: in order for Medicare to continue to pay for short-term rehab costs, the senior must **either be getting better or getting worse**. Once a person's medical condition is stable, they come off the Medicare reimbursement schedule and must pay for **all** costs.

Be careful, because even though there is up to 100 days of coverage, Medicare stops paying for most people in California around week three, or after 21 days.

From this point on, the patient will have to pay with their own money. The nursing home business office will advise you when this is expected to take place. **This is when you go from short-term rehab care to long-term care.**

If the facility where the short-term care was provided has long-term care beds, then the patient can stay where they are. But if there are no beds, the patient must find another facility for continued care or go home.

Be ready for this. Ask ahead of time if there are long-term care beds if you like the place you're sent to for your short-term care. If not, start looking right away for a facility that you do like.

Once someone goes from short-term to long-term care, how are they going to pay those unbelievably expensive monthly nursing home costs?

If they have long-term care insurance, it may pay some or most of the cost.

But, most people haven't bought long-term care insurance so they must either pay out of pocket or try to qualify for long-term care **Medi-Cal.**

Medicare = Short-term or rehab care
Medi-Cal aka Medicaid = Long-term care

KARL KIM, CFP®, CLTC

3 – What is Long-Term Care Medi-Cal?

The **only** government program that helps pay for nursing home bills for the middle class is called **Long-Term Care (LTC) Medi-Cal**.

It is not welfare!

Medi-Cal and Medicaid are the same program; Medi-Cal is California's version of Medicaid.

The rules, regulations, covered expenses, forms, etc., of Medi-Cal are all very confusing. Believe me, you will often feel like banging your head against the wall when dealing with the paperwork, staff, and business office of the facility.

Frankly, a lot of Medi-Cal just doesn't make sense. The program is a world onto its own. Not only is California's program different from that in other states, it fails to follow the law of common sense. That's why you can't go on the internet and easily find information about Medi-Cal.

This is also why CPAs, attorneys, social workers, and financial planners give out wrong information; they don't specialize in this area. Like everyone else, they mistakenly believe that the rules for all states are the same.

There is much misinformation and confusion out there, and it can even come from supposedly credible sources. There is a major Southern California newspaper that ran a column about Medi-Cal. The problem was that most of the important points were wrong and didn't apply to California.

But don't worry.

Within these pages you will get the **right information** for the state of California that is pertinent to your circumstances.

There is one more thing you need to know before we get into the details. There are two types of Medi-Cal: general Medi-Cal, and long-term care Medi-Cal. General Medi-Cal is for the uninsured who can't afford to pay hospital or doctor bills.

The qualification and administrative procedures are different for the two programs. We will be covering only long-term care (LTC) Medi-Cal. This is the program that helps pay nursing home costs.

4 – Doesn't Someone Have to be Broke to Qualify for Medi-Cal?

One of the more popular myths is that you have to be absolutely flat broke before you can qualify for LTC Medi-Cal. You may think you have to sell your house, spend all of your IRA funds, savings and investments before you can even think about applying. **This is absolutely NOT TRUE!**

What people don't know is that when it comes to assets, some things count and some things don't. **You will be absolutely astonished at what doesn't count!**

An asset can be countable or non-countable (non-countable means exempt or unavailable).

Medi-Cal determines your eligibility based on how much you have in **Countable Assets.**

Countable assets include anything that can be readily turned into cash. For example:

- Checking accounts
- Savings and money market accounts
- Time deposits or certificates of deposit
- Mutual funds
- Annuities
- Life insurance cash values
- Second car, motorcycles, trailers, motor homes
- Real estate other than your home, vacant land, time shares, vacation homes, rental real estate
- Retirement accounts **(if no income is being paid out)**

How Much Can a Single Person Have?

A single person can have no more than $2,000 in **countable assets.** This has to be achieved by the end of the month of application.

For example, let's say that you are applying for January. Your countable assets must be less than $2,000 by the **end** of January. The proof typically consists of a statement(s) from your financial institution(s).

It doesn't matter how many names are on an account. As long as the applicant's name is on it, 100% of the account is counted.

For example, let's say that mom has a $30,000 bank account with her two daughters. All $30,000 is mom's not just one-third (or $10,000).

It also doesn't matter if the account is in the name of mom's living trust. Medi-Cal views the account as mom's.

As we will cover later, living trusts offer no asset protection for Medi-Cal.

How Much Can a Married Couple Have?

If one spouse is applying, a couple can have no more than **$117,920** in countable assets for 2013. This number changes every year.

Just as in the case of a single person, it doesn't matter whose name is on the account or asset. For qualification purposes, all countable assets are added together.

The obvious question is why is a married couple allowed to keep more than a single person?

The answer is that the government feels a single person doesn't need any assets if they are in a nursing home.

On the other hand, the spouse at home needs to pay for groceries, insurance and utilities. Therefore, they are allowed to keep more in assets.

There is an additional $20,000 exemption for Japanese Americans interned during World War II.

What is an EXEMPT Asset?

An exempt asset **doesn't count**. Regardless of the value of the asset or account, it doesn't count.

An **"Exempt Asset"** is your home, regardless of its value. Whether you live in a mobile home or a mansion in Beverly Hills, it doesn't matter.

Here's the situation. Mom, who is a widow, is in a nursing home. She lived in her home for 55 years before going to the nursing home.

Realistically, she is never going to go home, but she would if she could, right? So this is the intent to return home.

As long as this **intent to return home** is established in writing, the home is an Exempt Asset.

This is why you need to have knowledge of the regulations specific to California.

It's that simple.

Now, when the Medi-Cal application is filled out, there's a question that you have to answer the right way to make sure that her home doesn't count as an asset; in other words, to make sure that it is exempt.

If you check the wrong box, Medi-Cal will make you sell the home, spend all the money on her care, and then re-apply.

This is what you don't want to happen. There is right way to fill out the tricky and confusing forms, and most importantly, save the family home. In addition, you should know the following:

- One car is exempt. It could be a $100,000 car or a $5,000 van. If it is mom's vehicle, it doesn't count.

- Burial insurance (otherwise known as a pre-need plan) is exempt. You can have the simplest of arrangements or a lavish going away celebration. If the irrevocable beneficiary is the mortuary, it doesn't count.

- o You must be careful here. In California, the correct (non-countable) pre-need contracts are sold only through mortuaries. Don't forget, the irrevocable beneficiary has to be the mortuary.
- o Pre-need plans sold by insurance agents are **not exempt** in California. Your plan must be purchased through a cemetery or mortuary.

- One burial plot is exempt, and Medi-Cal will request copies of the deed and purchase contract.
- Term life insurance is exempt because it has no cash value. Just make sure that there is a person assigned as beneficiary. Medi-Cal can recover against this policy if there is no beneficiary or if a living trust is the beneficiary.
- Cash value life insurance is exempt if the face amount is $1,500 or less. If the policy or policies exceed that amount, then the entire cash value counts.
- Jewelry such as wedding rings are exempt.
- Household goods and personal effects are exempt.

What is an UNAVAILABLE Asset?

Unavailable assets don't count.

Hold on to your hats because what you are going to hear is going to blow you away!

And it is **LEGAL!**

It is simply "knowing the rules."

The largest unavailable or non-countable asset for many applicants will be their retirement accounts, including IRAs, Roth IRAs, 401(k), 457, and 403(b)s **if an income is being taken on a regular basis.**

Here's an example of how this works. Let's say that a 55 year old, employed aerospace engineer has a health care crisis and is applying for Medi-Cal. He has $400,000 in his 401(k) plan. Because he was still working and contributing to his plan, the $400,000 is a countable asset.

Fast forward to the future.

Let's say that now he is a 75 year old retired aerospace engineer, has $400,000 in his IRA Rollover account and is applying for Medi-Cal. The IRS says that at no later than age 70 ½ he must take a Required Minimum Distribution (RMD).

For Medi-Cal qualification, his $400,000 IRA Rollover account is now unavailable and **doesn't count** for qualification.

In addition, suppose that he is married to a CEO of a large company and that she has $1,000,000 in her 401(k) plan. Because she is the spouse, the $1,000,000 in her retirement plan doesn't count, even if she isn't taking a distribution.

Unbelievable?

Yes! Did we do anything illegal?

NO! It is simply "knowing the rules."

What people don't know is that it isn't how much you have, but how those assets are arranged.

But what about the income from the IRA?

Well, that would be considered income for the applicant. For a 75 year old, the annual RMD that has to be taken according to IRS regulations is $17,467.25 or $1,456.00 monthly.

This income would be used to help pay the monthly nursing home cost. This is called the Share of Cost (SOC). Medi-Cal would pay the rest.

One of the problems that applicants may encounter is if a bank has multiple CDs in your IRA account with different account numbers but is taking the RMD from just one CD.

This makes the other CDs in the IRA countable assets. Medi-Cal frequently has denied cases as being over limit because of this.

5 – How Much Income Can Someone Have?

This topic can get very confusing. But because you can take the time here to re-read this chapter as needed, we'll give you the skinny.

Don't get discouraged if you don't understand everything the first time. Just go very slowly through the material.

Just as there are rules about assets and Medi-Cal qualification, the government has regulations in place so that a man or woman who is at home doesn't have to live like a pauper just because his or her spouse is in a nursing home.

But, unlike assets – that are combined for a married couple – income for married couples is separated. Everything depends on whose name is on the check. This is known as the **"Name on the Check Rule."**

We are also talking about income that cannot be *"turned off"* such as Social Security, pensions, or Required Minimum Distributions.

For example, the husband's name **only** is on his Social Security check. In this case, the income is **his**, and his alone.

The same is true for the wife's Social Security check. If her name **only** is on her check, the income is **hers** alone.

All of the income that is in the at-home spouse's name **only does not** affect the eligibility of the person who is applying.

The only income that affects the eligibility of the applicant is the **income that is in the name of the applicant only.**

Here's a little known secret. There is no limit to the amount of income that the at-home spouse can have. For example, let's say that the at-home spouse is a retired school teacher with a monthly pension of $6,000. Her name only is on the check.

Unbelievably, this does not affect the eligibility of her husband for Medi-Cal. Even better, she does not have to use any of her income to help pay for his nursing home care.

She gets to keep 100% of her pension!

There is no maximum income limit for qualification for Medi-Cal. But, if the applicant's income is more than $4,500, as a rule of thumb, it may not make sense to apply for Medi-Cal.

For a married couple, the spouse at home is allowed to have a **minimum** monthly income of $2,898 (for 2013). This is called the Minimum Monthly Maintenance Needs Allowance (MMMNA). The MMMNA changes annually.

This allowance gives the spouse enough money to pay household expenses. The government doesn't want the at-home spouse to be living in poverty just because their spouse is in a nursing home.

Let's take a look at an example of how this would work.

Joe is the applicant. His monthly income is:

Source	$ Monthly
Social Security	$ 1,200.00
Pension	$ 1,576.00
TOTAL	$ 2,776.00

Susan is the at-home spouse. She gets a monthly Social Security check for $1,000.

That's less than $2,898. Therefore, Susan is allowed to keep $1,898 of Joe's monthly income ($2,898 - $1,000 = $1,898.00).

Joe is also allowed, under Medi-Cal, to keep $35 as a personal needs allowance. We call this "toothpaste money."

All Susan pays each month to the nursing home for Joe's care is $843. This is called Joe's Share of Cost (SOC). Medi-Cal pays the rest.

Here's a chart to show how this would work.

Susan's Minimum Income	$	2,898.00
Susan's Social Security	$	(1,000.00)
Additional Income Needed	$	**1,898.00**

Joe's Gross Monthly	$	2,776.00
Income to Susan	$	(1,898.00)
Personal Needs Allowance	$	(35.00)
Monthly Payment to NH*	$	**843.00**

*NH refers to Nursing Home.

If, for example, the facility charges $7,000 per month, and Joe pays only $843, then Susan saves $6,157 each month (that's 88%). Don't you think that makes a huge impact on her life?

(Please note that Medi-Cal uses gross income before taxes, insurance and other deductions to calculate your income.)

Did you get that? Remember, what you need to understand from the previous example is that the spouse who is at home will be able to maintain his or her standard of living.

Let's take a look at another example. Joe has the same monthly income of $2,776.

Now, let's give Susan more income. Her monthly Social Security check is $1,000 and she has a pension income of $2,000.

The key here is to remember that both of these checks are made out to Susan **in her name only.** So, all of this is Susan's income and it is separated from Joe's income. Her income doesn't affect Joe's eligibility for Medi-Cal benefits.

Susan's total monthly income is $3,000. This is greater than $2,898 so she doesn't get to keep **any** of Joe's income.

Once again, because her name only is on the pension and Social Security checks, she keeps 100% of her income. None of it has to be used to help pay Joe's nursing home bill.

Each month, Joe's Share of Cost to the nursing home is $2,776 minus $35 (Personal Needs Allowance) for a total of $2,741. Medi-Cal pays the difference.

Susan's Minimum Income	$	2,898.00
Susan's Social Security	$	(3,000.00)
Additional Income Needed		–

Joe's Gross Monthly	$	2,776.00
Income to Susan		–
Personal Needs Allowance	$	(35.00)
Monthly Payment to NH	**$**	**2,741.00**

Remember what we covered earlier – for married couples, the "Name on the Check" rule applies. If Joe's name only is on the check, then that is his income only. If Susan's name only is on the check, then that is her income only. Joint income is divided equally.

The important point to remember is that the at-home spouse is not going to go broke and be forced to live on the street after paying for their spouse's nursing home costs.

Up to now we've only talked about married couples. For a single person, Social Security, pension and/or Required Minimum Distribution income is used to pay the Share of Cost. A single person still gets to keep the toothpaste money of $35.

This is why in an earlier statement, we said that LTC Medi-Cal is not welfare. The person on Medi-Cal has to use their income to help pay for their nursing home costs. It is not a free ride.

The rules do allow a person to protect their assets for their spouse or family. But you have to know the rules!

KARL KIM, CFP®, CLTC

6 – Paperwork, Paperwork: The Application Process

When is the application submitted?

Many people think they can apply for Medi-Cal at any time. This is **not** the case.

Someone has to actually be in a nursing home before the application can be submitted. An LTC Medi-Cal worker will call the facility to make sure that the applicant is really there.

Also, the facility has to be Medi-Cal approved. Not all nursing homes are. Check with the business office of the facility where you are planning to go and make sure they are Medi-Cal certified before the patient is transferred.

It is a good idea to prepare everything ahead of time (if possible) because there are a lot of supporting documents that must be submitted.

Remember that LTC Medi-Cal is a government program – so there is lots and lots of paperwork. There are two applications: a long and a short. Some counties only use the long application and some use both.

Los Angeles County only uses the long application. Orange County uses both. The short application can be printed from the Medi-Cal website:

(http://www.dhcs.ca.gov/services/medical/Documents/PDF _Medi-Cal%20Applications/English/English%20Application.pdf).

By submitting the right applications from the start, at least two weeks processing time can be saved.

You don't have to be an attorney to submit a Medi-Cal application. At present, the only state that we are aware of that requires an attorney to prepare the forms is Texas.

A spouse, adult child, relative or friend can sign the application as the Authorized Representative. Don't worry. This is only so they know who to mail the notices to. There is **no** financial responsibility attached to this.

Be careful about allowing the business office of the nursing home to submit the application. They will do so for free, but down the road this may end up being a very costly mistake.

Many people go through the application process once in their lifetime. The forms are confusing and there are alligators in every question. Do it right the first time, and you won't regret it later.

Another advantage of engaging a professional is to handle the myriad of phone calls that Medi-Cal workers love to make. You sign one form, and that allows the professional to speak to the Medi-Cal workers on your behalf.

This is a good choice because it takes the stress off of people so they don't have to worry about saying the wrong thing or checking the wrong box. The professional takes care of everything from start to finish: qualification, follow up, approval, separation of accounts, Recovery avoidance, annual redeterminations, and Recovery notices.

This is where the rubber meets the road. There aren't a lot of companies or individuals that actually submit and follow up on applications.

Many attorneys love to prepare the trusts and other documents, but will not submit a Medi-Cal application. The reason is that the process is very time consuming, often confusing, and very frustrating. The approval of the case rests in the hands of the Medi-Cal worker who is assigned to it.

The professional's goal is to make the LTC Medi-Cal worker's job as easy as possible. Because the applications are organized and complete, clients get approved faster.

The following items need to be gathered before the application can be submitted.

Information to be submitted ✳

As with other government programs, the amount of paperwork to fill out is overwhelming. The only thing a professional can't do is gather the necessary items. This is the only thing that the spouse or family has to do.

Submitting an application that is organized and complete results in the quickest possible approval. Because a professional knows what Medi-Cal needs, a little more time should be taken to make it easier for the Medi-Cal worker to review the case.

The following list is what is needed to complete an application. If the applicant is married, information for **both** husband and wife are required. It is not just the applicant who must provide the following. Copies are fine.

- Social Security card.
- Medicare card.
- Health insurance card.
- Valid California Senior ID card or Driver's License. If none is available, then a recent utility bill in the applicant's name will suffice.
- Birth Certificate. If none is available, then a voter registration card will be applied for.
- Resident Alien card or naturalization certificate.
- Current facility information such as name, address, and phone number.
- Most recent health insurance bill showing name of insured, premium amount, and frequency of payment.
- Payment stubs or statements showing gross pension, RMD, or other income.

- *"Your New Benefit Amount"* from Social Security that comes in December and shows the next year's monthly benefit.
- Previous 4 months of bank statements, including closed accounts. All pages must be provided even if blank.
- Previous 4 months of brokerage, mutual funds or other investment account statements.
- Life insurance, annuity policy, and most recent statement showing face amount and cash value for each.
- Burial trust policy paperwork, including contract.
- Vehicle registration.
- Deed for burial plot.
- Deed and tax bills for all real estate.
- Living trust, including Schedule A.

Keep copies in a place where they can be easily accessed in time of crisis. Also, keep a copy of the Durable Power of Attorney for Asset Management and Advanced Health Care Directive handy.

It doesn't have to be fancy. Use a big cardboard box and throw all these items into it. At least you'll know everything is in one place.

How long does it take for the application to be approved?

Medi-Cal has *45* days to either approve or deny the case.

We recommend using UPS Overnight or Fed Ex to send in your application. This way you know exactly when the application was received and when the clock started ticking.

Here's an interesting, yet little-known fact. Let's say that your father has been in a nursing home for a while. But you thought that he didn't qualify for Medi-Cal.

After reading this book you learn that he does qualify. He can get benefits for up to 3 months prior to the month of application.

For example, let's say that Joe entered the facility on June 1st. He was financially qualified but his family did not submit the application until September 15th.

The application was not approved until October 30th. Joe's Medi-Cal benefits will be retroactive to June 1st.

If Joe's family had been private-paying from June 1st, they would be entitled to a refund of the difference between the SOC (Share of Cost) and what they had paid.

This could be really useful if someone is tight on money.

What happens when Medi-Cal receives your application?

Every county does things a little differently. Los Angeles County, because it's so big, gives out only the long application. They also prefer to handle the entire process through the U.S. mail.

Some smaller offices prefer in-person applications. Others work with phone or mail or both. Just about all start out with the short application. They will send out the other forms later.

When an office starts with the short form, we submit both the short and long. This saves a week or two of processing time.

When Medi-Cal gets your application, they look at both **assets and income.** They take a "financial snapshot." Something is either an asset or income. That's it. There's no in-between.

In Los Angeles County, your application goes to the Assignment Desk first. From there, it is assigned to a case worker within a few days.

The application typically sits in a drawer for a few days. The case worker then quickly goes over it. If more information is needed, a form is mailed out requesting it.

The authorized representative then has one week to get everything back to the case worker. But, there is an automatic 5 day extension if more time is needed.

Medi-Cal goes through everything with a fine-tooth comb. The experience of the worker who is assigned to your case determines the outcome here. In any event, the more complete the paperwork is, the faster the application is approved.

Sometimes things go smoothly, and sometimes they don't. Always try to be as cooperative and helpful as possible. This really helps to get the application approved as quickly as possible.

Once everything is in and looks good, the worker approves the application. All data is entered in a computer. The file is then transferred to a supervisor for final approval.

How much do I pay to the nursing home while the application is being processed?

Usually, the facility will ask you to pay the normal rate. Once the application is approved, they will give a refund or credit.

Some will ask for an initial deposit, for instance, of $5,000. They will then wait until the application is approved. Most nursing homes are for-profit companies and have bills to pay.

The professional can perform an initial calculation of the Share of Cost then ask the facility to accept this, rather than the "normal" rate.

You must always pay at least the Share of Cost while the application is pending.

7 – You're Approved! Now What?

CONGRATULATIONS! After all of that hard work and stress, your application has been approved.

Unfortunately, Medi-Cal doesn't send you an approval letter. What you receive is a **Notice of Action**. This Notice of Action is mailed out from the local Medi-Cal office once final approval is given.

What the Notice of Action indicates is the month your benefits begin and what your Share of Cost (SOC) is. The SOC is how much you have to pay the nursing home each month.

A "Benefits Identification Card (BIC)" is also mailed. This is a white card with your identification number and effective date on it.

The business office of the facility typically will want a copy of the card.

For a single person, there is nothing further to do.

In the case of a married couple, there is additional work to be done. This involves separating accounts within 90 days of the approval date.

The name of the person on Medi-Cal has to be taken off of all accounts. The only account that they will have is a checking account.

The spouse's name and/or the adult children can also be on this account. This is the account where the Social Security, pension, and other income are deposited.

From this account, the Share of Cost, premiums for health insurance, drug coverage, and the spousal allowance – if any – are paid.

From this point forward, the spouse on Medi-Cal can have no more than $2,000 at the end of each month.

Here is what very few people know.

Unbelievably, the at-home spouse can now have an unlimited amount of assets.

For a married couple **assets are treated separately** once the spouse has been approved. The at-home spouse can win the Mega Millions jackpot and this will not disqualify the spouse on Medi-Cal.

The at-home spouse must have their own accounts where their Social Security and other income will be deposited.

8 – The Annual Redetermination

You must reapply for benefits every year.

But don't panic!

The annual redetermination is not nearly as intense as the original application process. However, it has to be done a couple of months before the anniversary date.

With the annual redetermination application, the most recent bank statement also needs to be included. (If married, **both** spouses' statements are required.)

In addition, any pre-need contracts, the *"New Benefit Amount"* statement from Social Security and any other account statements need to be sent in. If the home has been quit claimed, include a copy of the new deed.

The countable assets for the person on Medi-Cal needs to be under $2,000. The at-home spouse is allowed an unlimited amount of assets. The reason that all statements are required is so that the Medi-Cal worker can calculate the Share of Cost and reallowance for the at-home spouse.

If everything is in order, there is no Notice of Action sent. In other words, no news is good news.

9 – Medi-Cal Wants
Their Money Back

Think of Medi-Cal as a loan to help pay nursing home costs while someone is alive.

But after that person passes away, the State of California wants their money back. This process is called:

Recovery

Fortunately, there are simple, legal and straightforward methods for avoiding Recovery. But you have to know about Recovery ahead of time.

The whole key to avoiding Recovery is to have as little as possible in the estate of the person that was on Medi-Cal at the time of death.

Typically, the uneducated get trapped when it comes to their home.

Remember back to the qualification section – the home doesn't count as an asset for approval.

What a lot of people don't know is that the home is not exempt from RECOVERY!

Not knowing this could cost your family a lot of money. Recovery bills can range from $800 to $167,000 to over $300,000!

If you know what to do, your family can bring this down to $0.

What needs to happen is that while the person on Medi-Cal is alive, the home needs to be transferred to either the at-home spouse, in their name only, children or other beneficiaries.

Because the intent to return home was established in writing when the application is filed, the home is an **exempt asset**.

Exempt assets can be transferred at any time, to anybody, with no penalty.

Why do you want to do this? So the State cannot recover against the home. As long as the home is out of the Medi-Cal person's name at the time of their passing, Medi-Cal cannot go after it (even if it is in the children's name).

To be safe, an attorney should file the quit claim or transfer.

This is where California is different from the rest of the country. Not only does California allow a penalty-free transfer after approval, they also allow a penalty-free transfer before application.

Now, when the person passes away with no home in their name and as little cash in the bank as possible, the most Medi-Cal could get is the cash in the bank.

However if this cash is used for funeral expenses, then they probably will get nothing.

Let's take a look at an example. A person can qualify for Medi-Cal with a home (exempt) regardless of its value and have less than $2,000 in the bank.

Let's say that the mom has been on Medi-Cal for 10 years and has a bill of $300,000 to the State. At time of her death, she owns a home worth $300,000 and has $100 in the bank.

The Recovery department sends a bill to her son. He has 60 days to pay the $300,000.

Does he have $300,000 lying around? Probably not.

If he can't pay the bill, the State will place a claim on the home for $300,000.

He is now forced to sell his mom's home. He nets $300,000 from the sale. This $300,000 goes to the State.

This is not what mom or son had in mind.

How could this have been avoided? Let's suppose that mom had quit claimed the home to her son while she was alive and on Medi-Cal.

Now when she dies, her estate at time of her death is valued at $100. Her son uses this $100 to help pay for her funeral expenses and saves the invoice.

He gets a bill from the State for $300,000. He sends the department a copy of her last bank statement showing the balance of $100 and the funeral expenses invoice for $1,000.00.

Medi-Cal then sends him a letter saying that they will not file a claim against his mom's estate. In other words, he owes nothing.

Isn't that a better ending?

Remember earlier we said that you should never let a nursing home file the Medi-Cal application for you even though they will do it for free?

This is the reason. The nursing home will not help to avoid RECOVERY! *NB*

All the nursing home cares about is getting paid. NOW!

And as we have seen, Recovery bills can get huge!

Be aware that there are tax issues when you transfer an interest in real property while you are living, so be sure to consult your tax advisor. If you are having an attorney do the transfer, the attorney will also advise you about property and other tax issues.

There are simple yet effective strategies for avoiding Recovery and protecting your assets for your spouse and family, but you have to plan properly.

Let me ask you a question. What if the person on Medi-Cal is legally incapacitated due to Alzheimer's and cannot sign the quit claim? How would you take that person's name off of the home?

Keep reading and you'll find out.

10 – Your Most Important Estate Planning Document

We are **not** attorneys.

However, we work with a network of attorneys that we have known for a long time. They are estate planning attorneys who specialize in wills, trusts and probate, and also have a good knowledge of Medi-Cal.

What we will cover in this chapter is not to be construed as legal advice because only an attorney can give legal advice. We will be describing the issues and solutions that we have seen.

The first thing you need to know is that all wills and trusts are not alike. Just because an attorney is licensed doesn't mean that they are Medi-Cal knowledgeable.

There is specific language that must be included in your documents. These cover a wide range of Medi-Cal situations that a traditional estate planning attorney may not be familiar with.

Having the proper estate planning documents is an essential part of the Medi-Cal and retirement planning process.

So the question that we asked earlier was:

If someone cannot sign a quit claim to take their name off of the home, what can the spouse or family do?

Once again, it all goes back to knowing about Recovery.

Early on, a Durable Power of Attorney for Asset Management (financial) should be prepared. This will allow the attorney-in-fact – (or spouse or child(ren) for example – to remove the person's name from the home if they cannot sign or do not have capacity.

The Durable Power of Attorney is the **most** important estate planning document that you can have. This will help to avoid Recovery and protect assets for the spouse and family.

The Durable Power of Attorney for Asset Management should also allow gifting in excess of the annual exclusion, which is currently $14,000. This situation would occur if we were to gift the home to an adult child, for instance, or to decrease excess countable assets in the case of a single person.

It should also include language so that your representative can apply for Medi-Cal for you.

Here's another little known fact:
Living trusts offer no protection from Medi-Cal.

Having the right type of revocable living trust is also important for a husband and wife. A Disclaimer trust is what my attorneys recommend rather than an A/B or A/B/C trust.

A disclaimer trust gives the surviving spouse (upon the death of the first spouse) the option to keep all of the assets in one pot rather than two pots (A/B trust).

Keeping the assets in a single trust gives the surviving spouse the flexibility to move assets around in order to qualify for Medi-Cal.

Dividing the assets into an A/B trust is most often done to minimize estate taxes, but makes it difficult or impossible for the surviving spouse to move assets around in order to qualify for Medi-Cal.

As we have discussed, in the case of a husband and wife, once approved, all accounts must be separated. If there are bank, credit union, brokerage or other financial institution accounts titled in the name of the trust, these accounts are going to have to be closed because in the eyes of Medi-Cal, these are joint accounts.

Therefore, the existing living trust will be revoked and a new trust will be established for the at-home spouse.

Should the at-home spouse pre-decease the Medi-Cal spouse, the assets should go down to the beneficiaries and not sideways back to the Medi-Cal spouse.

The power to revoke the existing trust by the at-home spouse should also be included.

We've covered a lot of ground in here and this is not meant to be a one-size-fits-all chapter.

We hope that you now know that you have to see the right kind of attorney, one that is Medi-Cal knowledgeable, or work with a financial planner that is.

Hopefully you also see the importance of having the proper estate planning documents in place as soon as possible. You never know when a health care crisis will occur!

11 – Mysteries of the Look Back Period Revealed

In California, the **"Look Back Period"** is especially confusing. Even professionals have difficulty in this area.

For most of the country, the look back period is 60 months (5 years), but in California it is **30 months (2 ½ years)**.

What exactly is the Look Back Period? Isn't it the penalty period? If I make a gift within the look back period aren't I ineligible for Medi-Cal? If I give my home away, don't I have to wait until the look back period runs out?

These are all common questions. It just shows all of the misinformation floating around out there. So let's get to the bottom of it.

The term "Look Back Period" simply refers to the period of time before the application is submitted.

When filling out the Medi-Cal application, the State asks if you've given anything away to someone other than your spouse, or transferred anything for less than fair market value within 2 ½ years (30 months) prior to the month of the application.

Husbands and wives can give each other as much as they want without incurring a penalty.

But what happens if a gift is made to someone other than a spouse during the look back period?

Well, it all depends.

It depends on how much the gift was for.

It also depends on when the gift was made.

Just because a gift is made within the look back period, doesn't automatically mean that someone is disqualified.

Let's take a look at a few examples of how this works.

Let's say that mom is in a nursing home. Her son is submitting an application in the month of September.

She gave him $10,000 2 years ago in September.

So is she disqualified? Let's walk through the calculation to figure out whether she is or not.

First, we divide $10,000 by the 2012 Average Monthly Private Pay Rate (APPR) of $7,092. This gives us 1.41 months.

California rounds down so 1.41 rounds down to 1 month. Therefore. she is ineligible for one month the month of September.

Next, we have to determine when the gift was made. Looking at a copy of the check, we see that she wrote the check on September 1st, 2 years ago.

Because her penalty was one month, she is disqualified only for the month of September, 2 years ago. The gift has no effect on her application today.

Did you follow that? If you didn't, go back and read it again.

Let's do another. Say that she gave her son $106,500 2 years (or 24 months) ago. Isn't she disqualified? Well, let's figure it out.

Divide $106,500 by $7,092 (the APPR) and we get 15 months. Because 15 months is less than 24 months, she is eligible for Medi-Cal.

Did we just do anything **illegal**?

NO! It was just knowing the rules.

Let's do one final one. What if she gave her son $595,728 2 years ago?

$595,728 divided by $7,092 equals 84 months (or 7 years).

Because she applied 2 years after she made the gift, and it is within the look back period, she is disqualified for 5 more years (5 more years plus the 2 years she has already waited) for Medi-Cal benefits.

What should her son have done instead?

He should have waited 7 more months, and then applied.

Here's why: there is no period of ineligibility for gifts or transfers made **outside** of the look back period regardless of the amount.

For example, an aunt gave her nephew $1,000,000 3 years ago. If she applies for Medi-Cal today, she does not have to disclose this gift as it was outside of the look back period of 2 ½ years.

Unbelievable but true!

Gifts can come in many different ways. For example, mom has a CD with her name and her daughter's name on the account.

The CD matures and when she renews it, she takes her name off the CD and leaves it in her daughter's name only. That's a gift.

Dad has a second home with a market value of $400,000. He sells it to his son for $100,000. That's a gift of $300,000.

Mom writes her son a check to reimburse him for the home care services that he paid on her behalf. She has all of the receipts and copies of her son's checks.

This is not a gift because she can justify the reason and amount for the check (home care reimbursement).

Dad has a second home with a market value of $400,000 and has the comparisons to prove it. He sells the home to his son for $400,000. That **is not** a gift (he sold for fair market value).

What about the home?

Remember what we covered earlier about being sure to take the important steps to establish the intent to return home?

If you do this, then the home is an exempt asset.

Exempt assets can be transferred to anyone at any time with no penalty. For Medi-Cal purposes, the transfer of an exempt asset is **not** a gift.

So there is **no** penalty, even if the transfer occurs during the look back period.

What about taxes?

Many people are also confused when it comes to taxes. They have heard that the most someone can give away in a year is $14,000. They also think that someone has to pay income tax on the gift.

Well, part of that is true. The most someone can give away in a year is $14,000 **without filing a gift tax return**.

So let's say that a father gives his son $20,000 in a year. The father has to file a gift tax return for $6,000.

This is simply notifying the IRS that he gave away $6,000 more than the $14,000 for a year.

There is no income tax for either father or son.

As of 2013, a person can give away up to $5 million while they are alive with no income or gift tax to either party.

Why is all of this important?

Because this is the cornerstone to getting a single person qualified who would otherwise have too much in countable assets.

12 – How to Qualify With Excess Countable Assets

Medi-Cal has only two categories for an applicant's finances.

Something is either **income** or an **asset**.

As we have learned, irrevocable income can't be turned off. So if someone has too much income, they may not want to apply.

But if someone has too much in countable assets, there are ways to get qualified.

Single Person

How much over $2,000 in countable assets do you have?

The answer determines the best strategy to use. Excess funds can always be spent down with no penalty on **exempt** assets.

For example, if you need to fix the roof of your house, you can. If you need to put in a yard sprinkler system, you can. If you need to paint the house, you can. Excess countable assets can be spent without penalty.

You can buy a car if you don't have one or trade in the one you have and get a van. Excess countable assets can also be used.

Purchasing an irrevocable pre-need burial plan with a mortuary is also okay. Excess funds can also be spent on purchasing a burial plot or niche.

Funds can also be spent on medical expenses, home care, medications, medical equipment, and doctor and hospital expenses.

Be careful because you **cannot** private pay for nursing home care to bring your assets down for the month that you are applying for Medi-Cal. You can, however, pay the Share of Cost.

Here's where California's treatment of gifts made within the look back period is different from the rest of the country.

As we learned earlier, gifts or transfers made within the look back period are assessed a penalty that is based on the amount of the gift and when it was made.

Every gift that is made in the look back period stands on its own. That means that each penalty also stands on its own; nothing is added together.

This is a good thing. It allows people to protect more assets for their families and qualify for Medi-Cal as early as possible.

Let's take a look at an example. A father has $86,000 too much in countable assets to qualify. The month is September.

He can write a check for $86,000, but that would mean that he would have to wait for 12 months before applying.

Here's what we would advise. We would tell him to make a gift of $34,000 in September. He is ineligible for Medi-Cal for four months, or September to December.

He makes a gift in October of $24,800. He is ineligible for October to December.

He makes a gift in November of $17,700. He is ineligible for November and December.

Finally, he makes a gift in December of $9,500. He is ineligible for December.

Assuming that he has under $2,000 of countable assets by the end of January, he would be eligible for Medi-Cal beginning January 1st.

He transferred a total of $86,000 with only four months of ineligibility using our method – versus having made a lump-sum payment of $86,000 in September.

This can be done only in California. This is why Medicaid/Medi-Cal is so confusing to people.

Married Couples

For married couples, we are going to use three rules that we previously covered.

The first is the "Name on the Check" rule. Income that is only in the name of the spouse at-home isn't counted for the applicant.

The second is the rule that there are only two categories when a financial snapshot is taken: Income or Asset.

Third, the at-home spouse can have any amount of assets after approval.

For example, the husband is in a facility and the wife is the at-home spouse. They have a total of $300,000 in countable assets and have $182,080 too much for the husband to qualify.

We can protect **100%** of the excess countable assets for the wife and family. The husband will qualify for Medi-Cal **immediately**!

Here's how. The secret is that the excess countable assets are converted into income. So now we just moved it from assets to income, and made it legally disappear.

That income is paid to the wife **in her name only**. Because of the "Name on the check" rule, she doesn't have to use that income to pay for her husband's nursing home care and she keeps 100% of it.

She keeps 100% of the excess countable assets!

In addition, this income is irrevocable, just like a pension. All of the monies are paid monthly to her for approximately five years.

Because spouses can transfer unlimited amounts of money between themselves with no penalty, the husband qualifies immediately for Medi-Cal.

Should she pass away before he does, the beneficiaries are the children. So, the children would receive the monthly payments until they are completely paid out.

The moral of the story is that you **don't** have to spend down all of your assets in order to qualify for Medi-Cal benefits. There are ways to protect most, if not all of them, for your spouse and family.

Closing

CONGRATULATIONS!

You made it through. Our hope is that you understand the Medicare and LTC Medi-Cal system in California just a little bit better than you did before. It is a very confusing subject. You aren't alone in that feeling.

We know that you are reading this book because someone in your life is dealing with this issue right now or is soon to be.

Remember that the financial side of this is very important, but choosing the right level of LTC services, finding the right caregivers, etc. are also important factors.

One final note is that you have to remember that the information in this book is current as of the date it was written in 2013. As we stated earlier SB483 was signed into law, but has yet to be implemented.

That's why it is crucial that you get on our email list so that you can be notified if there are any changes and how they may affect your family.

You can also go to our website www.KarlKimCo.com and watch our blog posts.

For more information, please send an e-mail to Karl@KarlKimCo.com.

38164909R00035

Made in the USA
San Bernardino, CA
06 September 2016